W9-BKA-278

I Love Gymnastics!

By Jane Feldman

A Random House PICTUREBACK® Book

Random House 🏠 New York

Hi, my name's McKenzie. I am seven years old and live in Riverdale, New York. I love to rollerblade, play with friends, and go to the movies. But my most favorite thing to do is…

gymnastics!

This is my mom and me. She thinks I'm a very good gymnast. She always tells me that if I practice hard enough, I could be one of the best! If you ask me, I think she's the best mom in the entire world.

When I'm not in school, Mom lets me practice my gymnastics in our yard. See, this is me about to do a handstand.

And this is me practicing an elbow bridge. Doing a bridge is very hard. I always make sure to stretch out really well before trying one.

I love going to the beach to collect seashells and starfish. But no matter where I am, the one thing I always want to do is gymnastics.

I think it's really neat to practice and hear the ocean behind me at the same time. I also like feeling the sand press up against my bare feet.

One of the great things about gymnastics is that it has six different forms. They're called rhythmic, artistic, trampoline, tumbling, sport acrobatics, and sport aerobics.

In rhythmic gymnastics, I use cool things, like a ribbon or a hoop. I think the ribbon looks so pretty when it twirls through the air.

That's me and Wendy Hilliard, who is my terrific rhythmic coach. Even though I work really hard with her, we always have a great time together.

The hoop is my favorite part of rhythmic gymnastics because I think it's neat to spin it around. It takes a lot of coordination.

But spinning can get pretty tricky, and I sometimes
lose my hoop! Whenever that happens, Wendy tells me
I better keep practicing!

Sometimes I take classes at the Sutton gym, where I practice artistic gymnastics.

I love going to the gym because there's lots of fun equipment to use.

That's Mimi. She's an instructor at the gym. She's teaching me the right ways to move so I don't get hurt.

Learning the right moves is very hard because there are so many angles and positions.

It takes lots of concentration and patience to get it right.

I used to think somersaults were easy, but Mimi has shown me that it takes a lot of practice to do them the right way. Especially backward somersaults!

The rings are so much fun, but they're also very hard. Only the boys are allowed to perform on them during a gymnastics competition. Mimi says I should do plenty of pull-ups to build my muscles. This way, I'll be able to show those boys a thing or two!

I love gymnastics! What other sport can you do upside down?

Out of all the exercises in gymnastics, the balance beam is the toughest for me. I have to do all my moves correctly while balancing on a narrow beam that's really high off the ground! I feel pretty proud when I do it perfectly.

One day, I hope to be such a good gymnast that I'm invited to the Olympic Games. I know it will take a lot of practice and hard work to get there, but I'm ready. Who knows, maybe I'll even win a gold medal!